The Roman Empire

LOUISE SPILSBURY

raintree

a Capstone company — publishers for children

Raintree is an imprint of Capstone Global Library Limited, a company incorporated in England and Wales having its registered office at 264 Banbury Road, Oxford, OX2 7DY – Registered company number: 6695582

www.raintree.co.uk
myorders@raintree.co.uk

ISBN 978 1 4747 7777 3 (hardback)
ISBN 978 1 4747 7785 8 (paperback)

British Library Cataloguing in Publication Data
A full catalogue record for this book is available from the British Library.

Acknowledgements
We would like to thank the following for permission to reproduce photographs: Cover: Shutterstock: Photolikkk: top; Wikimedia Commons: Diliff: bottom; Inside: Shutterstock: 79mtk: p. 21r; 7th Son Studio: p. 13b; Abxyz: p. 31; Antb: pp. 32–33; Bambambu: p. 29br; BeanRibbon: p. 43b; Benedictus: pp. 40–41; S.Borisov: p. 4–5; Valery Evlakhov: p. 27b; Vitaly Fedotov: pp. 24–25; Gerald Robert Fischer: p. 39t; FlareZT: pp. 18–19; Eric Isselee: pp. 13r, 41br; Kentaylordesign: p. 14–15; Olga Meffista: p. 16t; Mountainpix: pp. 5b, 37r; Marco Ossino: p. 12; Regien Paassen: pp. 26–27; Pattang: p. 11br; Richard Yoshida: p. 7b; Wikimedia Commons: pp. 1, 8, 10–11, 44–45; 1803: purchased from Musée des monuments français: p. 34; Nicolas Beatrizet/ Bequest of Phyllis Massar, 2011: pp. 6–7; Roberto Bompiani/Digital image courtesy of the Getty's Open Content Program: pp. 36–37; Bristol City Council, Kurt Adams: p. 33br; Helen Cook: p. 9; Jusepe de Ribera: p. 19; Jean-Léon Gérôme: pp. 16–17, 20–21; Jun: pp. 28–29; Rolf Krahl: p. 25b; Poniol60: p. 15b; Hartmann Schedel: p. 45r; Ursus: p. 23b; WolfgangRieger: pp. 30, 38–39; Yeowatzup: pp. 22–23; Zde: pp. 35, 42–43.

Every effort has been made to contact copyright holders of material reproduced in this book. Any omissions will be rectified in subsequent printings if notice is given to the publisher.

Contents

CHAPTER 1

Rome: city of death

Around two thousand years ago, the city of Rome was at the centre of a huge **empire** that ruled more than one-quarter of the people on the planet. The Roman Empire was very creative and smart, but it was also cruel, bloodthirsty and murderous.

The city of Rome was founded, or built, on death. **Legend** says that Romulus and Remus, twin sons of the god Mars, were left to drown in a river by an evil uncle. They were rescued and raised by a wolf. As adults, the boys killed their uncle and then, Romulus killed Remus so that he could build a new city and call it Rome, after himself.

The Romans ruled their large empire with violence, too. Those who broke laws were often killed. There were vicious fights and other blood sports that not only entertained people, but also made them fearful. There are plenty of other horrors in Rome's long history.

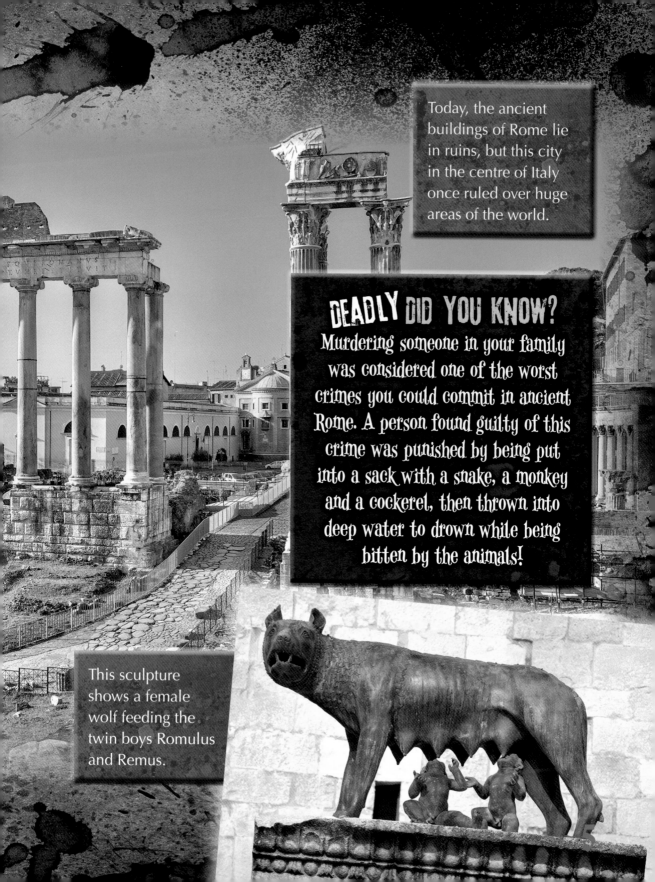

Today, the ancient buildings of Rome lie in ruins, but this city in the centre of Italy once ruled over huge areas of the world.

DEADLY DID YOU KNOW?

Murdering someone in your family was considered one of the worst crimes you could commit in ancient Rome. A person found guilty of this crime was punished by being put into a sack with a snake, a monkey and a cockerel, then thrown into deep water to drown while being bitten by the animals!

This sculpture shows a female wolf feeding the twin boys Romulus and Remus.

Cruel conquerors

Ancient Rome was a beautiful and wealthy place, but the **emperors** who ruled over it were greedy. They wanted more land and greater riches, so they sent their armies to **conquer** the world.

Rome's armies were the greatest killing machines that the ancient world had ever known. Roman soldiers fought with the most fearsome weapons and were so dangerous that they **defeated** enemies with armies ten times bigger than theirs.

Most people feared the sound of Roman soldiers' footsteps and **surrendered** immediately. Anyone who tried to fight back was tortured and killed. Roman armies killed millions of people and robbed thousands of cities before setting them alight.

A lot of Roman battles involved vicious fighting at close range.

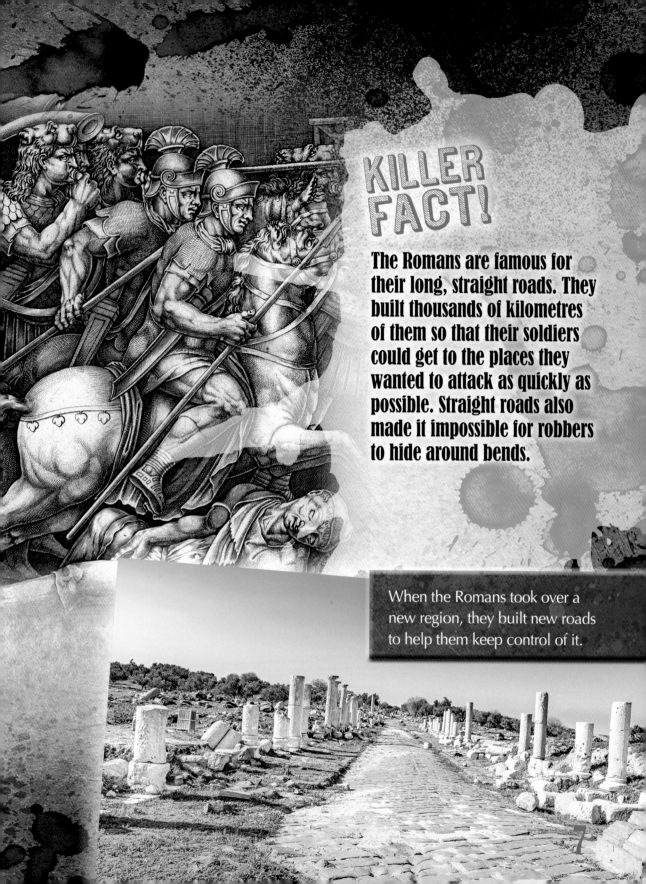

KILLER FACT!

The Romans are famous for their long, straight roads. They built thousands of kilometres of them so that their soldiers could get to the places they wanted to attack as quickly as possible. Straight roads also made it impossible for robbers to hide around bends.

When the Romans took over a new region, they built new roads to help them keep control of it.

Evil emperors

The emperors who ruled Rome did so with absolute power. Some were good and made changes for the better, but many emperors used their power for evil.

Emperor Nero allowed no one to stand in his way. He is famous for murdering his mother and two wives. Nero also tortured his best friend. He made ordinary people pay unfairly high **taxes** so that he could afford **luxuries**.

Emperor Trajan once ordered games that lasted 123 days. In them, pairs of men had to fight wild animals.

Many of the Roman emperors loved blood sports. They made men called gladiators fight one another in vicious, bloody fights to entertain crowds. Gladiators were often prisoners of war, **slaves** or criminals.

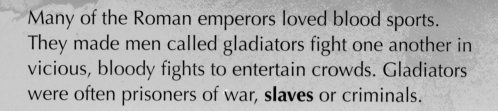

DEADLY DID YOU KNOW?

Emperor Nero blamed a terrible fire in Rome on the Christians living there. As punishment, he set fire to many of them, and used the burning bodies as evening lights.

Emperor Nero took money from ordinary people to build a marble and gold house with a 30-metre- (98-foot-) high statue of himself at the door.

CHAPTER 2

Bloody sports

When the Romans went to see a show at an **amphitheatre**, they wanted to see blood and violence. One sport that proved very popular was men fighting fierce wild animals such as lions and crocodiles.

Trained hunters wearing light body **armour** carried long spears to attack and fight the animals. As well as lions and crocodiles, they also fought leopards, tigers, rhinoceroses, elephants and giraffes.

The wild animals were kept in cages beneath the floor of the amphitheatre. They were lifted up and released suddenly into the arena through trap doors. When leopards, lions and tigers were in the amphitheatre, barriers were put in place to stop these dangerous animals leaping into the audience.

Animal fights were brutal, and up to ten thousand animals may have been killed in just one day.

The Romans were fascinated with and terrified by fearsome crocodiles.

KILLER FACT!

The wild animals were treated very badly before a fight. They were beaten and starved so they would be more vicious but also weak. This meant that the human hunters usually won.

Violent chariot races

The most popular Roman sport was the violent and bloody **chariot** racing. Bloodthirsty crowds loved these races because they were dangerous for the drivers and the horses that pulled the speeding chariots.

The chariot drivers and the horses were often badly injured or killed in their races.

The chariot races were not just about speed. Drivers tried to force other chariots to crash. The chariots were light, delicate and easily destroyed. Drivers were often thrown from their chariot. If they then became entangled in the long reins, they were dragged across the ground and under the chariots' wheels.

Spectators at chariot races behaved badly. Chariot drivers raced in teams of four different colours, each with its own supporters. This rivalry could lead to nasty fights in the stands. Emperor Vitellius, who supported the blue team, once ordered the **execution** of several spectators who called his team rude names.

DEADLY DID YOU KNOW?
Chariot drivers drank goat dung for energy. They boiled it in vinegar or ground up dry goat dung into a powder and mixed it into drinks.

Goats were valued for their meat – and also for their energy-giving dung!

Arena of death

The Colosseum amphitheatre in Rome was sometimes deliberately flooded with water. Then, brutal and gory sea battles were fought between men on boats.

These were huge events in which criminals were forced to fight to the death to re-enact real sea battles. Hundreds of them were killed in fights or fell into the water and drowned, all for the amusement of the cruel crowds.

Thousands of people queued up to see shows like this. At one event, people even slept in the street the night before to be certain of getting good seats. Some of them were crushed as crowds forced their way into the arena to watch the bloody show.

The Colosseum could seat around fifty thousand people who would come to watch the reenactment of famous battles that Rome had won.

KILLER FACT!

The trireme was a Roman warship that was powered by 170 oarsmen. It was tipped with a deadly bronze battering ram designed to puncture and sink enemy ships.

Roman triremes could be destroyed when battles were reenacted.

CHAPTER 3

Gruesome gladiators

ΜΑΡΓΑΡΕΙΤΗC

Thousands of Romans went to amphitheatres to see the gory sight of gladiators fighting one another in violent struggles. These games were bloody and brutal, and many gladiators died horrible deaths from their wounds.

Roman gladiators often fought with no protection on their chest, back or legs.

Different types of gladiators were forced to fight each other to make the games more entertaining. *Retarius* gladiators had a net to capture their opponents, whom they would then stab with a three-pronged **trident**. They often fought against *secutor* gladiators, who had a sword and wore a closed helmet with holes only for their eyes.

Crowds wanted to see gladiator fights with bloodshed and some sort of cruel, new twist.

Andabata gladiators were usually criminals who had been sentenced to death. They were given a horse but they had a helmet with no eye holes, so they charged their horses blindly at opponents to the great amusement of the bloodthirsty spectators.

KILLER FACT!

Gladiators who were too scared to enter the arena were hit with whips or prodded with red-hot iron rods to force them to fight.

Terrible training

Gladiators were trained under the eye of their owner in gladiatorial schools. These schools were surrounded by a **fortress** and were more like prisons. Gladiators lived in cells and their training was tough.

Gladiators came out to exercise, to train and to learn how to use their weapons. At one school, trainees were shown how to fight wild animals. Gladiators were also taught how to die because Roman crowds expected them to die gracefully and with honour.

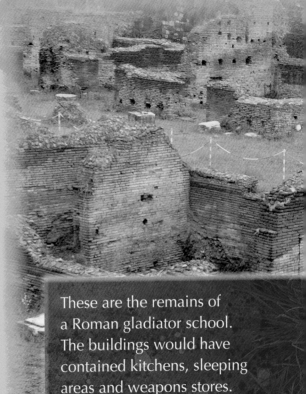

These are the remains of a Roman gladiator school. The buildings would have contained kitchens, sleeping areas and weapons stores.

Life must have been made even more unpleasant because of the food they were given. Gladiators were fed a lot of beans to build up layers of fat. It was thought this would protect them when they were hit, but they must have been very gassy. They washed down dinner with a drink made from plant ashes and vinegar, which was supposed to build up their bones.

Though female gladiator contests
were rare, the women probably fought
to the death, just like the men.

Doomed to die?

At the Colosseum, a typical day at the races included many deaths, all watched over by the emperor who paid for the games. He watched from a special seat where all the spectators could see him and he could enjoy watching the victims who were doomed to die.

Before gladiator fights in the afternoon, criminals and prisoners of war were pushed into the arena to be executed. Dangerous animals killed some of them. Others were forced to fight one another to the death. Some executions were set up to look like scenes from **mythology**.

Gladiators fought to the death – it was a case of kill or be killed!

When a gladiator was wounded in a fight, the emperor looked to the noisy crowd. If the spectators wanted the gladiator to live, they waved their handkerchiefs. If they put their thumbs down instead, the gladiator was killed immediately.

KILLER FACT!

Some gladiators survived more than one hundred fights. But words carved onto tombstones suggest that most gladiators died a painful death before they were thirty years old.

A gladiator's tombstone sometimes recorded the grisly way in which he died.

21

CHAPTER 4

Awful armies

Gladiator shows turned war into a game, but for Roman soldiers, fighting was a serious and horrible reality.

Each Roman soldier had two throwing spears, a short sword and a dagger. The spears had a sharp iron spike at the end. Soldiers threw these to kill enemies. They also threw them into enemy shields – pierced with spears, the shields were weighed down and made useless. This left the enemy open to attack.

Rome's soldiers were trained in tactics that made them almost impossible to beat.

The sword was light. It had sharp edges and a fearsome v-shaped tip. It was used for stabbing enemies because it could go through their armour and into their flesh. Daggers were worn on the belt and used to attack enemies if the sword was lost.

DEADLY DID YOU KNOW?
Roman soldiers carried a large shield that protected their whole body, making it very hard for enemies to hit or counterattack them.

Soldiers needed to be strong enough to carry their shields, which weighed about 10 kilograms (22 pounds).

Murderous machines

One reason Rome's army of 300,000 men became the greatest fighting force in the world was because of the murderous machines its soldiers used.

The *onager* resembled a giant, wooden catapult. It fired large stones or balls of burning tar, which could smash through walls and forts. Then soldiers could rush forward and kill enemies who thought they were safe inside.

Siege towers were large wooden towers that could be pushed up to enemy buildings. Soldiers inside the towers then attacked the enemy.

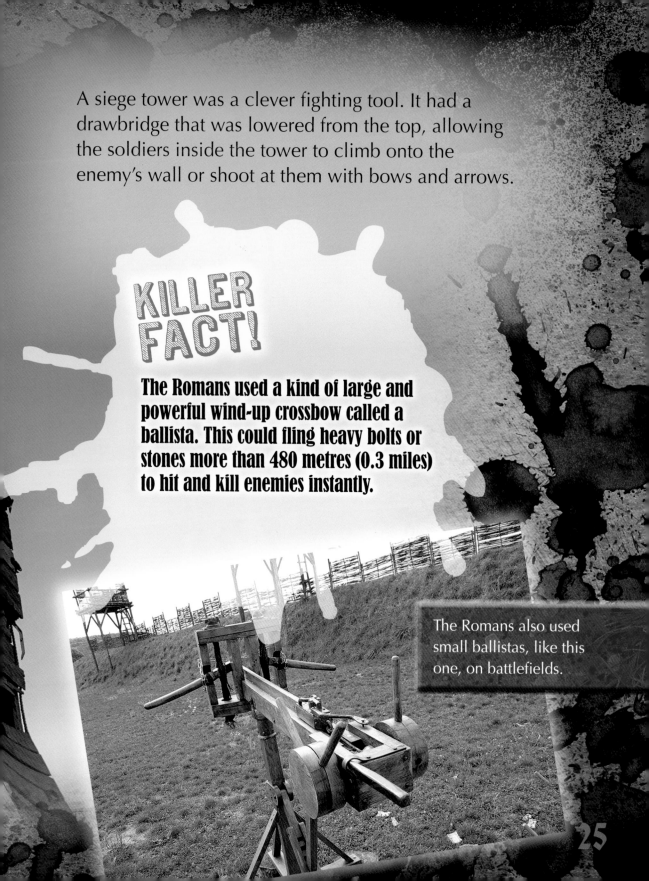

A siege tower was a clever fighting tool. It had a drawbridge that was lowered from the top, allowing the soldiers inside the tower to climb onto the enemy's wall or shoot at them with bows and arrows.

KILLER FACT!

The Romans used a kind of large and powerful wind-up crossbow called a ballista. This could fling heavy bolts or stones more than 480 metres (0.3 miles) to hit and kill enemies instantly.

The Romans also used small ballistas, like this one, on battlefields.

A soldier's sorrows

Roman soldiers faced great risks on the battlefield, but they almost always followed orders. If they disobeyed, they faced a harsh punishment.

Roman soldiers were divided into groups called legions. The legions were then divided into groups of one hundred soldiers. The centurion who led them carried a short rod. He would use this to beat any soldiers who disobeyed him. Soldiers who fell asleep on duty or behaved in a cowardly way were often executed.

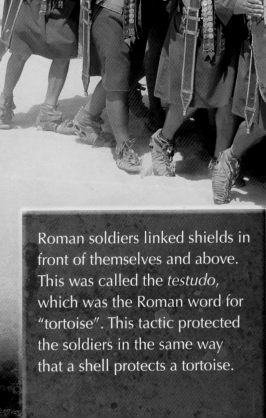

Roman soldiers linked shields in front of themselves and above. This was called the *testudo*, which was the Roman word for "tortoise". This tactic protected the soldiers in the same way that a shell protects a tortoise.

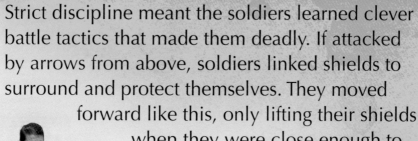

Strict discipline meant the soldiers learned clever battle tactics that made them deadly. If attacked by arrows from above, soldiers linked shields to surround and protect themselves. They moved forward like this, only lifting their shields when they were close enough to attack and defeat the enemy.

A bag of salt does not seem a great reward for risking life and limb in battle!

DEADLY DID YOU KNOW?

Roman soldiers were brutal killing machines. For their bloodthirsty work, they were paid in salt! The Latin word for salt was "sal". This is where the English word "salary" comes from.

CHAPTER 5

Long-suffering slaves

Roman armies sent thousands of captured soldiers back to Rome to be sold as slaves. Slaves became the property of their new owner and had to work for free. Some slaves were treated fairly, but others were worked to death.

Slaves were often badly treated and whipped. Those who tried to run away were branded – marked with a hot iron. Slave owners were allowed to kill slaves for any reason they chose.

Rich Romans might own as many as five hundred slaves.

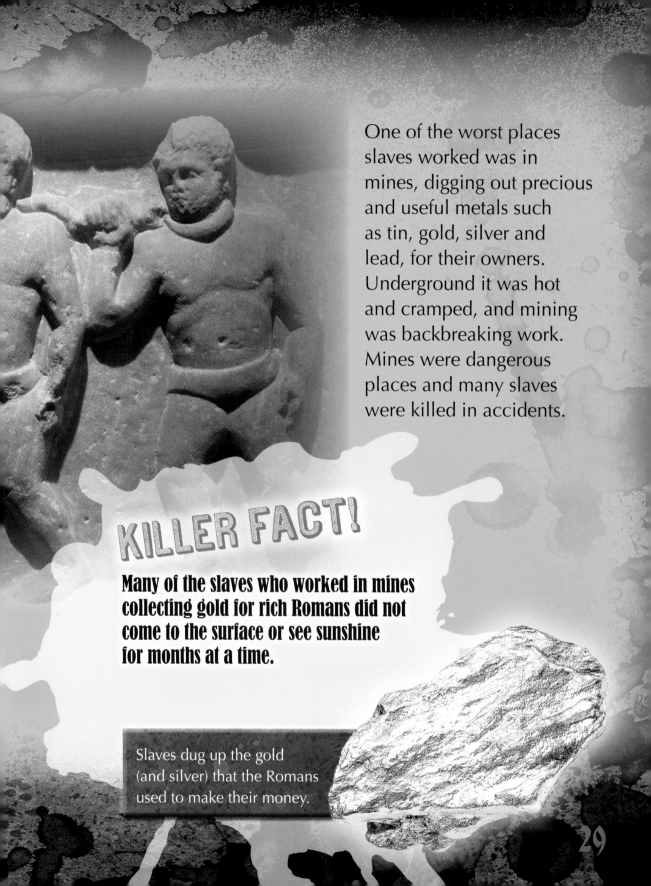

One of the worst places slaves worked was in mines, digging out precious and useful metals such as tin, gold, silver and lead, for their owners. Underground it was hot and cramped, and mining was backbreaking work. Mines were dangerous places and many slaves were killed in accidents.

KILLER FACT!

Many of the slaves who worked in mines collecting gold for rich Romans did not come to the surface or see sunshine for months at a time.

Slaves dug up the gold (and silver) that the Romans used to make their money.

Horrible jobs

Slaves did a lot of the work in Rome. While some worked as teachers, farmers, builders and even doctors, many were forced to do some really horrible jobs.

Some slaves were hairdressers. This was a less-appealing job than it sounds. Hairdressers had to use hair dyes made from ingredients such as pigeon **faeces**, rotting **leeches**, squid ink and urine.

Roman women spent a lot of time having their hair styled. Well-cared-for and styled hair was a sign of wealth.

Unpopular emperors lived in fear that their enemies would poison their meals. So they forced a slave to taste their food and drink before they did, to check if it was safe. Sometimes it was poisoned and some food tasters suffered excruciatingly painful deaths.

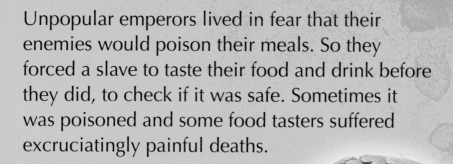

DEADLY DID YOU KNOW?
The slave Halotus is suspected of feeding Emperor Claudius a poisoned mushroom that killed him very quickly.

Emperor Claudius was a very unpopular emperor, so it is no wonder that his food was poisoned.

Beastly bath times

The Romans built amazing **aqueducts** that brought clean water to cities. They also built sewers to take away the dirty water.

To wash, the Romans visited bath houses with heated water. The bath house slaves had the horrible job of helping dirty Romans get clean. The unluckly slaves also had to rub dirty Romans all over with olive oil. The slaves then used a metal tool, called a *strigil*, to scrape off the filthy layers of dirt and oil from the skin.

Roman baths were large buildings that could hold many Romans and the slaves that had to help them wash.

The slaves that did the dirty laundry were known as fullers. To clean the clothes, they had to stand in tubs filled with water and substances such as stale urine, which had been collected from public toilets.

KILLER FACT!

Armpit pluckers were slaves who used tweezers to pull out hairs from stinky and sweaty Roman men's armpits.

The Romans thought that their armpits would not smell bad if they were hairless. They used tweezers such as these copper ones to pluck the hair.

CHAPTER 6

Horrible habits

The Romans had some truly horrible habits, from performing animal **sacrifices** and eating strange foods to wearing fabric with dye made from dead animals.

The Romans worshipped many different gods. They sometimes placed **offerings** for the gods on **altars** in their homes or at **temples**. Offerings included food such as fruit, milk or honey. The Romans also killed animals such as cattle, sheep, pigs and goats as gifts to the gods. Sacrificing dogs was thought to prevent crop diseases.

goat

A poor unsuspecting goat is taken to its death in a special sacrifice ceremony.

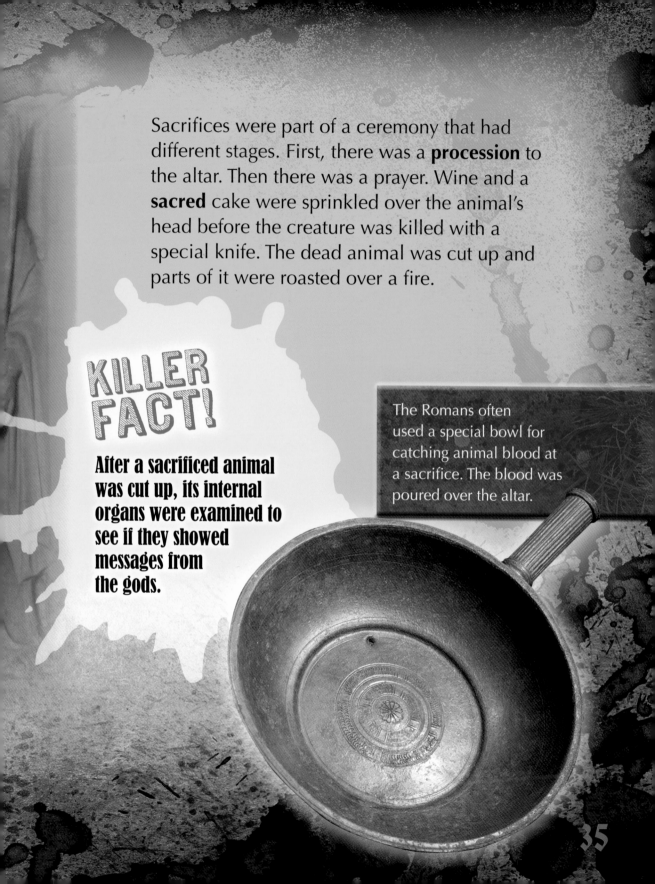

Sacrifices were part of a ceremony that had different stages. First, there was a **procession** to the altar. Then there was a prayer. Wine and a **sacred** cake were sprinkled over the animal's head before the creature was killed with a special knife. The dead animal was cut up and parts of it were roasted over a fire.

KILLER FACT!

After a sacrificed animal was cut up, its internal organs were examined to see if they showed messages from the gods.

The Romans often used a special bowl for catching animal blood at a sacrifice. The blood was poured over the altar.

Disgusting dinners

At banquets, emperors and very rich Romans wanted to show off their wealth by serving foods that were rare and expensive. These banquets could last for up to eight hours.

Some of the most unusual meals that rich Romans ate included peacocks' brains, flamingos' tongues and the heads of parrots and pheasants. One emperor liked to serve camels' feet and another had a taste for elephant trunks. One emperor even sprinkled pearls over his food instead of pepper.

Wealthy Romans were waited upon by slaves at mealtimes. The slaves poured drinks and carried food to and from the table.

When the greedy guests at Roman feasts were full, they did not stop eating. Instead, they made themselves vomit onto the floor or into bowls, which their slaves had to clear up. After vomiting, they would have space in their stomachs to eat more food.

DEADLY DID YOU KNOW?

Some rich people forced their slaves to run up mountains to fetch ice and snow, which were used to fill special wells and create a sort of fridge for storing their strange foods.

Slaves worked long and hard to gather enough food to satisfy greedy Roman appetites.

Festering fashions

Roman emperors wore purple to show how important they were. Purple dye was so expensive to produce that it was more valuable than gold. The colour may have looked beautiful, but the way Romans created it was quite horrible.

Purple dye was made by crushing thousands of small, rotting sea snails and leaving them to bake in the sun. Then they were boiled in giant lead pans for several days. The slaves who had the unpleasant job of making the dye had to suffer the terrible stench it created. The smell was so bad that dye-making workshops were built far away from the cities.

The slaves that made dye, coloured fabric and washed an emperor's clothes had a smelly and unpleasant job.

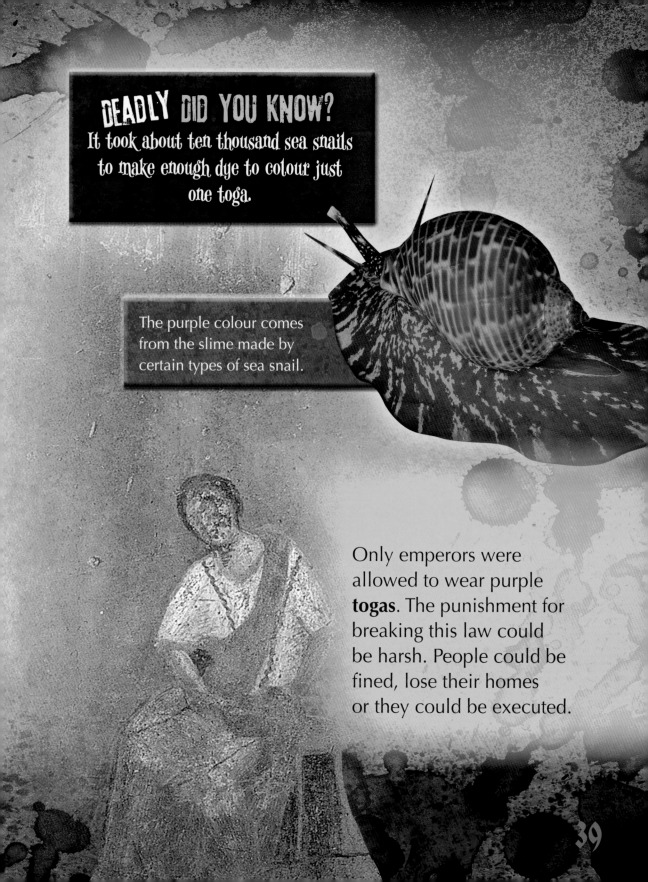

DEADLY DID YOU KNOW?
It took about ten thousand sea snails to make enough dye to colour just one toga.

The purple colour comes from the slime made by certain types of sea snail.

Only emperors were allowed to wear purple **togas**. The punishment for breaking this law could be harsh. People could be fined, lose their homes or they could be executed.

39

Toilet terrors

Rome was famous for its public baths, toilets and plumbing, but it was not always as hygienic or clean as it sounds.

Public toilets could be disgusting. Some Romans used special combs to remove body lice while they were sitting on the toilet. In fact, the toilets were rarely cleaned, so they were full of insects that would crawl up and bite people while they were sitting there.

Many people shared the public toilets and they also shared a sponge on a stick to wipe themselves afterwards. Like the toilets, this sponge was probably rarely cleaned. If the toilet germs did not kill them, people were sometimes blown up when methane gas from rotting human waste beneath the toilets exploded!

The Romans sat side-by-side while using the toilets.

Insects, such as this minstrel bug, were frequent visitors in Roman toilets – and their unexpected bites could be painful!

Death and disease

The gruesome discovery of the skeletons of forty-seven babies and children in Lugnano, north of Rome, revealed another horror from the empire's history. These young children and babies were all killed by the disease **malaria**.

This carving shows a family mourning the tragic death of their child.

Malaria spread easily because people travelled around the empire and because foreign **invaders** attacked Rome. The disease killed so many people in Rome that it became known as "Roman fever".

The Romans tried various medicines to cure their diseases. There are reports of people collecting the blood of dead gladiators and selling it as a medicine. Some Romans seemed to believe that drinking gladiator blood would cure certain conditions. Some people went one step further – they pulled out a dead gladiator's liver and ate it raw!

KILLER FACT!

Mosquitoes thrived in the marshy damp land around Rome, and malaria was spread when infected mosquitoes sucked on human blood.

A female mosquito sticks a straw-like part of her mouth through skin to suck blood.

A violent end

The Roman Empire began to fall apart in the fifth century. Some say that the Roman Empire ended much as it began – with blood and violence.

Rome's power was weakened by a series of useless emperors and bloody wars between different parts of the empire. Tribes such as Goths, Huns and Vandals from northern Europe took advantage of this weakness and started energetic and brutal attacks.

These invaders destroyed many of Rome's great buildings, stole its valuables and made many of its inhabitants slaves or murdered them. In AD 476, the last Roman emperor was forced to step down from power and a German prince made himself king of Italy.

The Vandals were a tribe that attacked and destroyed parts of Rome.

DEADLY DID YOU KNOW?

Rome named the invaders who attacked them barbarians. Roman soldiers greatly feared the heavy battleaxe weapons used by barbarians from Germany because these could smash through their shield, armour and helmet in a single blow!

Attila the Hun was one of the fiercest barbarian rulers who attacked the Roman Empire.

Glossary

altars tables or platforms on which religious rituals were carried out

amphitheatre oval or circular building with stepped seats around an open central space for spectators to watch contests and races

aqueducts artificial channels and bridges that carry water long distances for people to use

armour clothing worn by soldiers for protection

battering ram weapon that consists of a large wooden beam with a head of iron, which is used to beat down walls

chariot two-wheeled vehicle pulled by horses

conquer use force to take over a city or country

defeated beaten

emperors male leaders or rulers of an empire

empire large area of land or group of countries ruled over by one leader

execution killing of someone when given the order to do so

faeces digestive waste

fortress large, strong building that can be defended from attack

invaders people, armies or countries that use force to enter and take control of another country

leeches bloodsucking creatures

legend story from ancient times that is not always true

luxuries things that add to pleasure or comfort but that are not absolutely necessary

malaria disease spread by mosquitoes

mythology traditional stories about gods and heroes

offerings things that people give as part of a religious ceremony or ritual

procession group of people moving along in an orderly way, especially as part of a ceremony

sacred important to a religion

sacrifices animal or human that is killed to honour a god or gods

slaves people who are owned by other people and have to obey them

surrendered gave up or admitted defeat in battle

taxes money paid to a ruler or government

temple building where people go to worship their god or gods

toga loose outer garment worn by people in ancient Rome

trident three-pronged spear

Find out more

Books

Ancient Rome (History Hunters), Nancy Dickmann (Raintree, 2016)

Daily Life in Ancient Rome (Daily Life in Ancient Civilizations), Don Nardo (Raintree, 2016)

DKfindout! Ancient Rome, DK (DK Children, 2016)

Geography Matters in Ancient Rome, Melanie Waldron (Raintree, 2015)

Life in Roman Britain (A Child's History of Britain), Anita Ganeri (Raintree, 2015)

The Roman Empire and its Impact on Britain (Early British History), Claire Throp (Raintree, 2016)

Websites

www.bbc.com/bitesize/articles/z2sm6sg
Learn more about life in ancient Rome.

www.dkfindout.com/uk/history/ancient-rome
Find out more about ancient Rome.

Index